Balloon Animals

by Donna Freitag

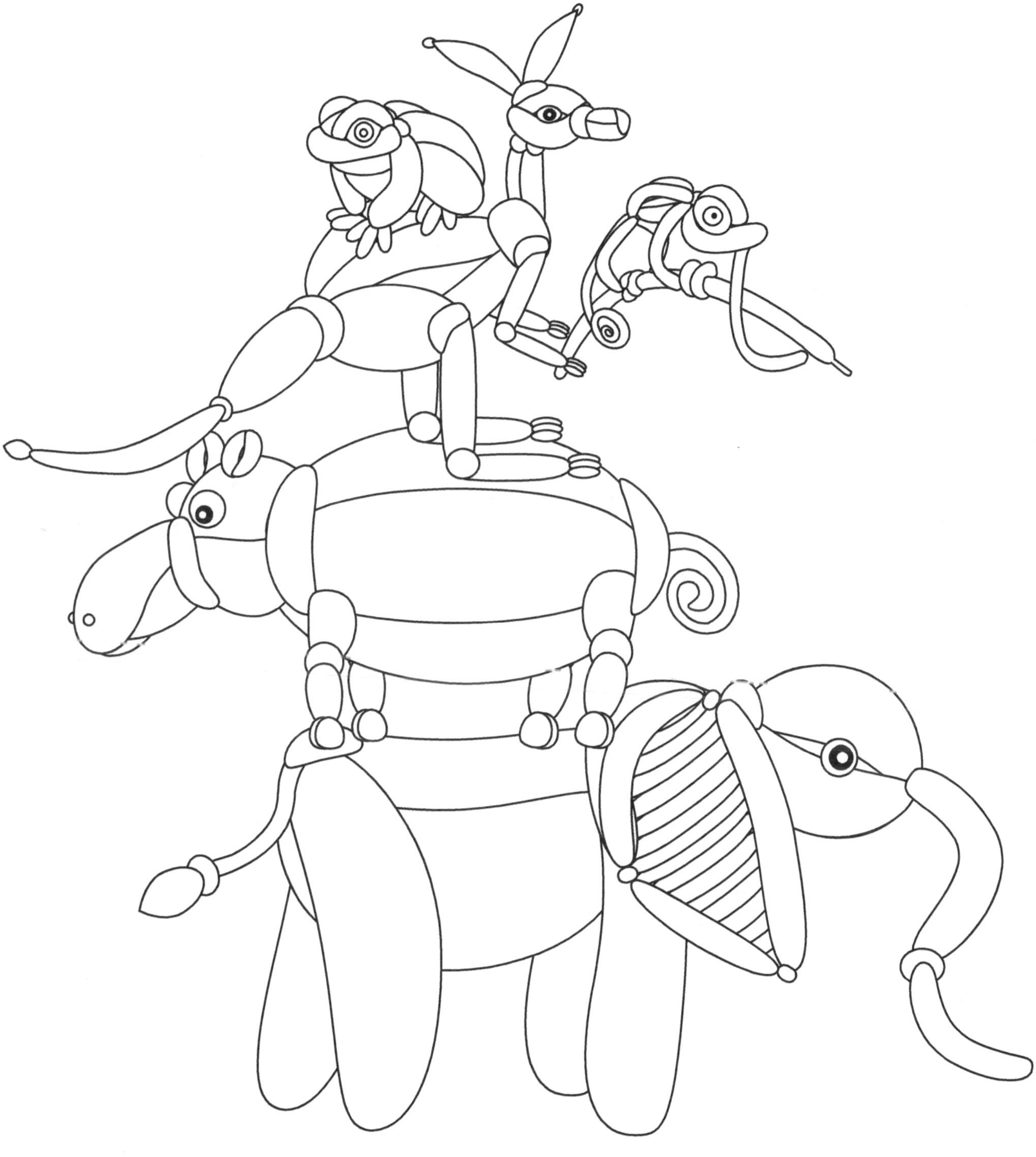

I0481425

Donnafreitag.com

How to color this book

Balloon Animals is a coloring book for adults. You'll enjoy hours of creative, relaxing, stress relieving fun as you color 27 all new balloon animal designs. All are beautiful, new, original artwork never before seen in any collection.

Coloring Tips

Colored pencils are the most popular way to color. It's best to get a large set of at least 48 colors. Some of the best brands are Prismacolor and Staedtler.

In addition, you'll need an eraser and a good pencil sharpener. Also popular are markers. Warning: they tend to bleed through the page. So if you use them, place a sheet or thick paper underneath so the ink doesn't leak onto the picture below. Copic markers are a great brand.

Marker sets offer a smaller choice of colors than pencil sets. That's one reason why the pro colorists often use a combination of pencils, markers, gel pens and even crayons.

It all depends on the effects you want to produce.

Please post photos of your artwork on my Facebook page. I'd love to see what you've done!

Be sure to follow us on social media...

f donnafreitag90

y @donna_r_freitag

◉ @donnafreitag1991

p donna_freitag

Join our mailing list for the latest news and freebies.

Visit www.donnafreitag.com

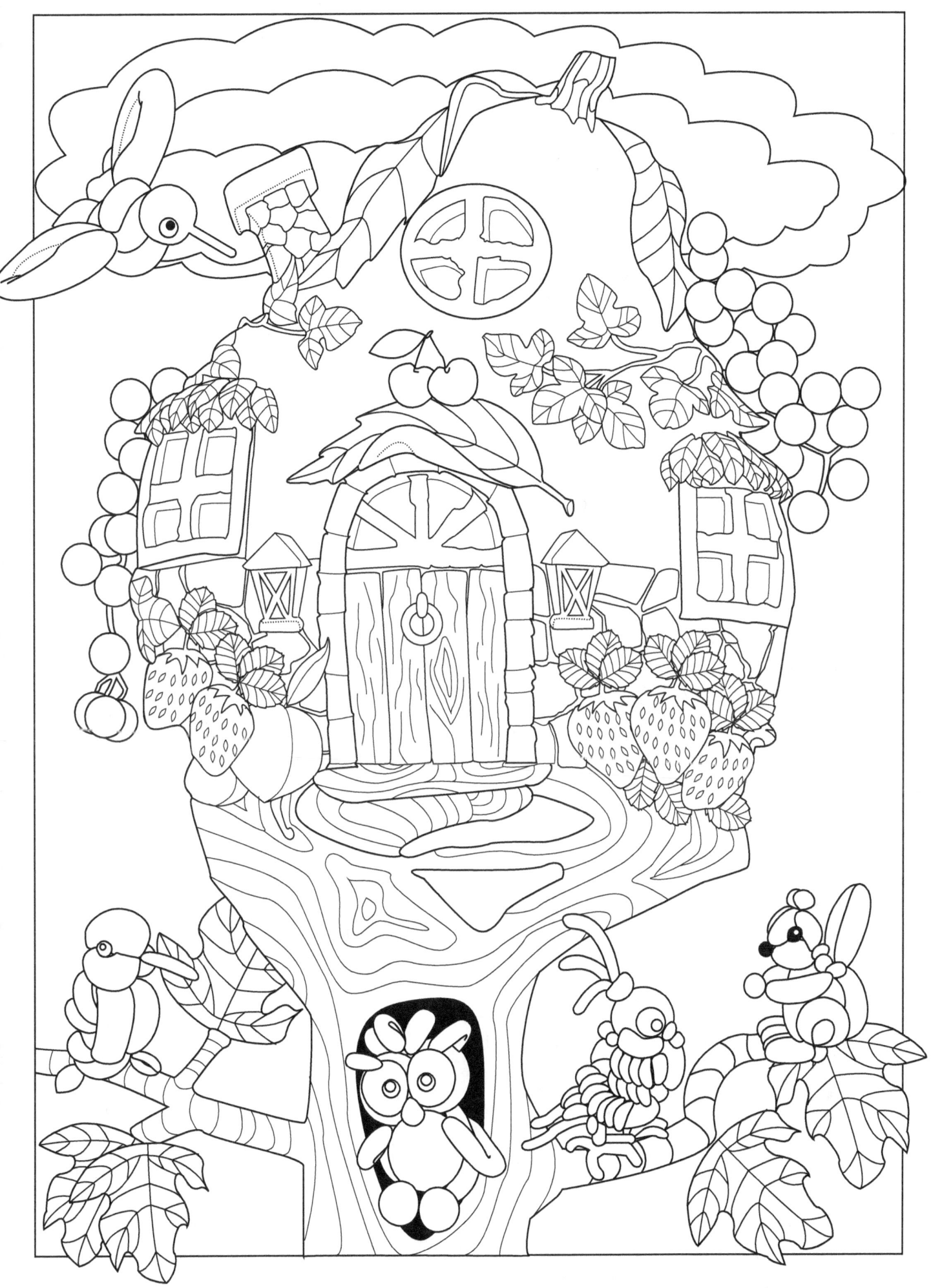

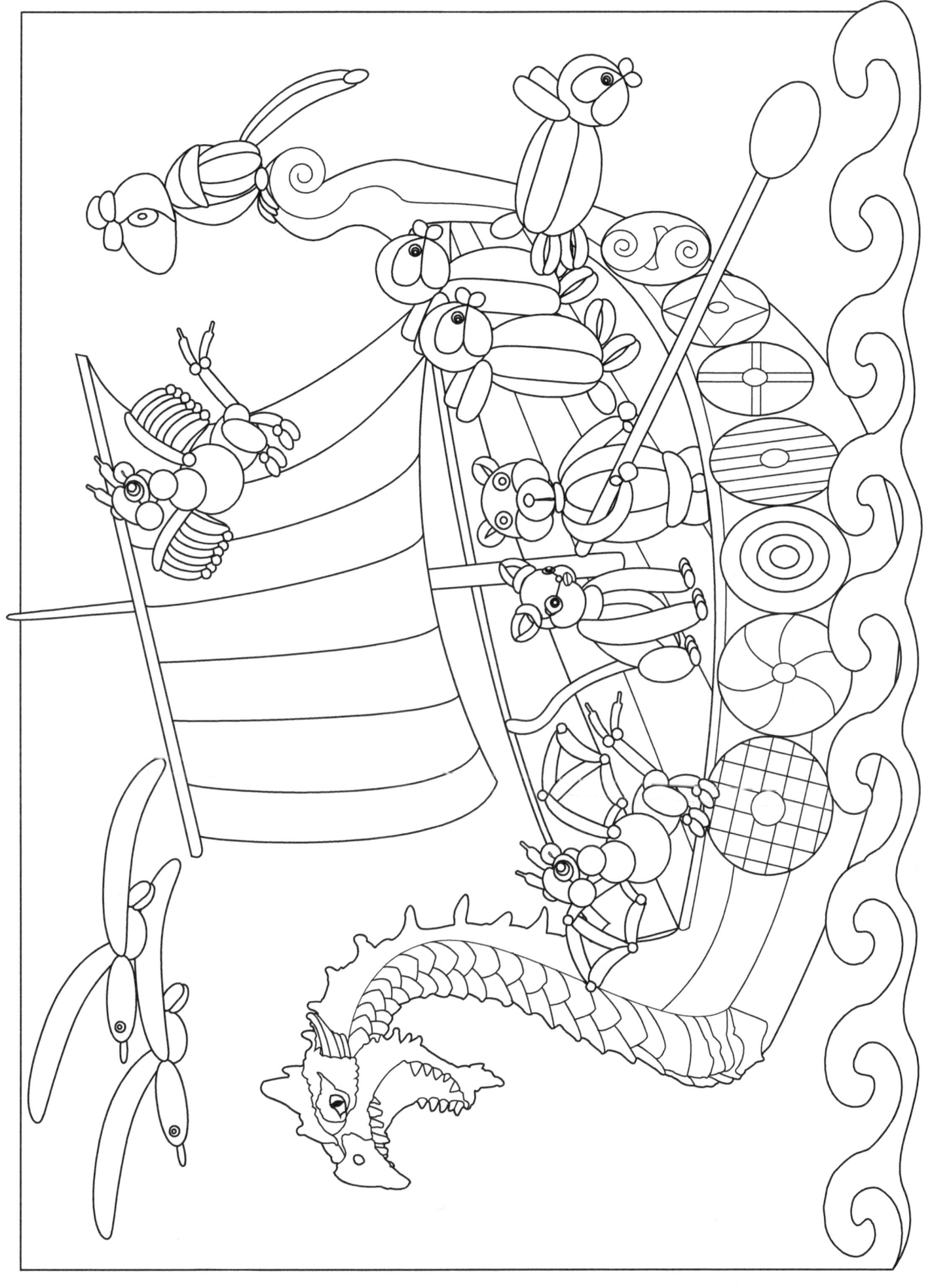

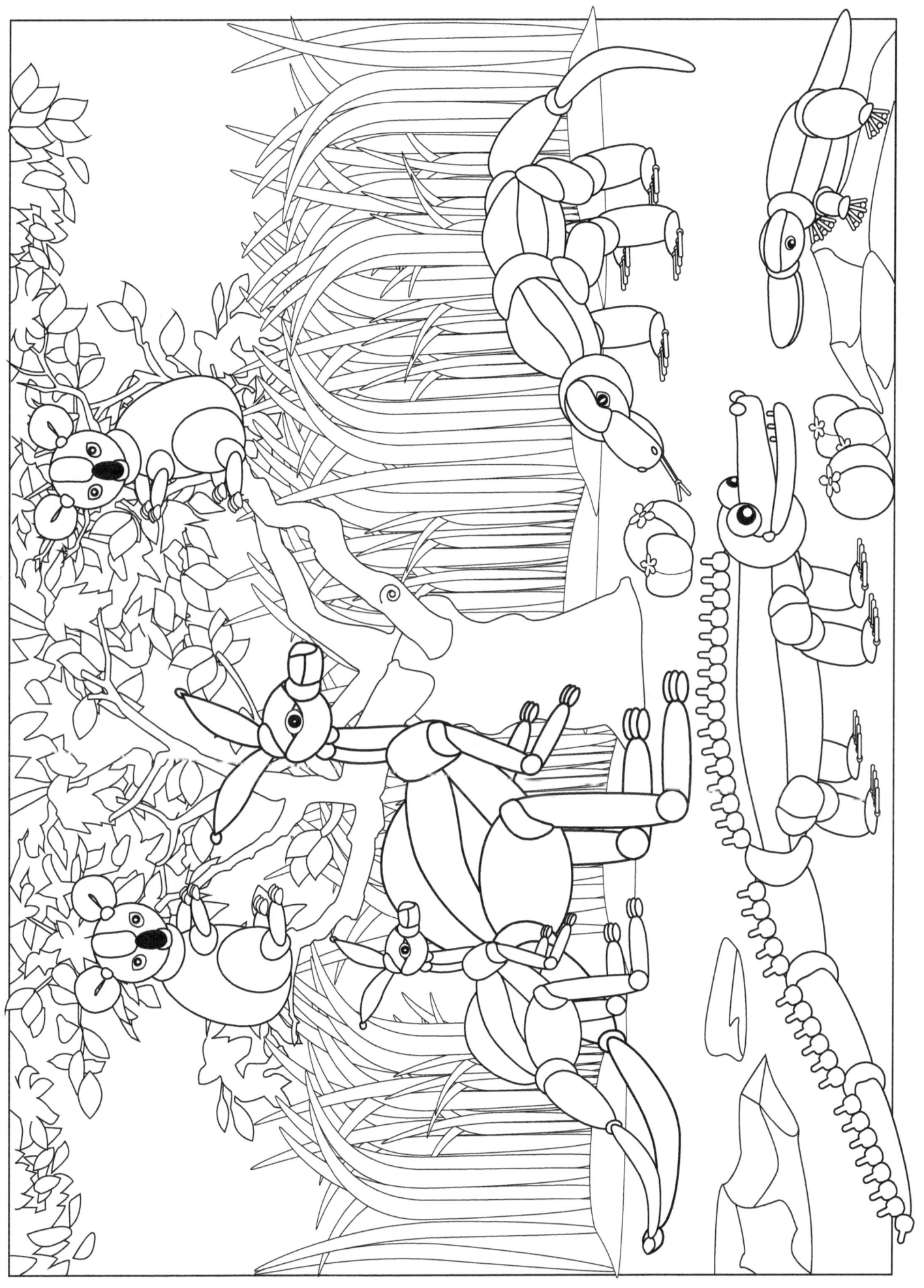

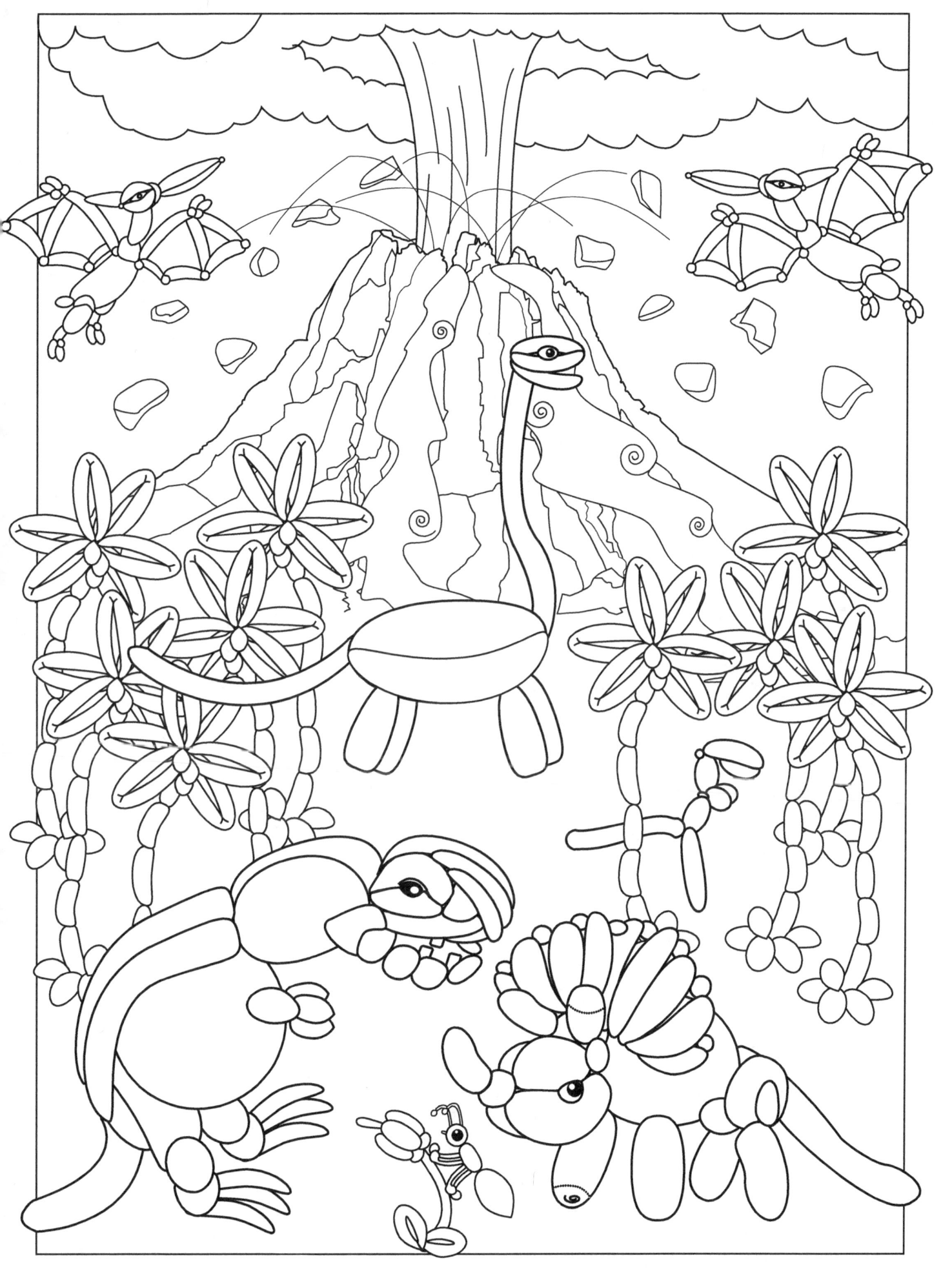

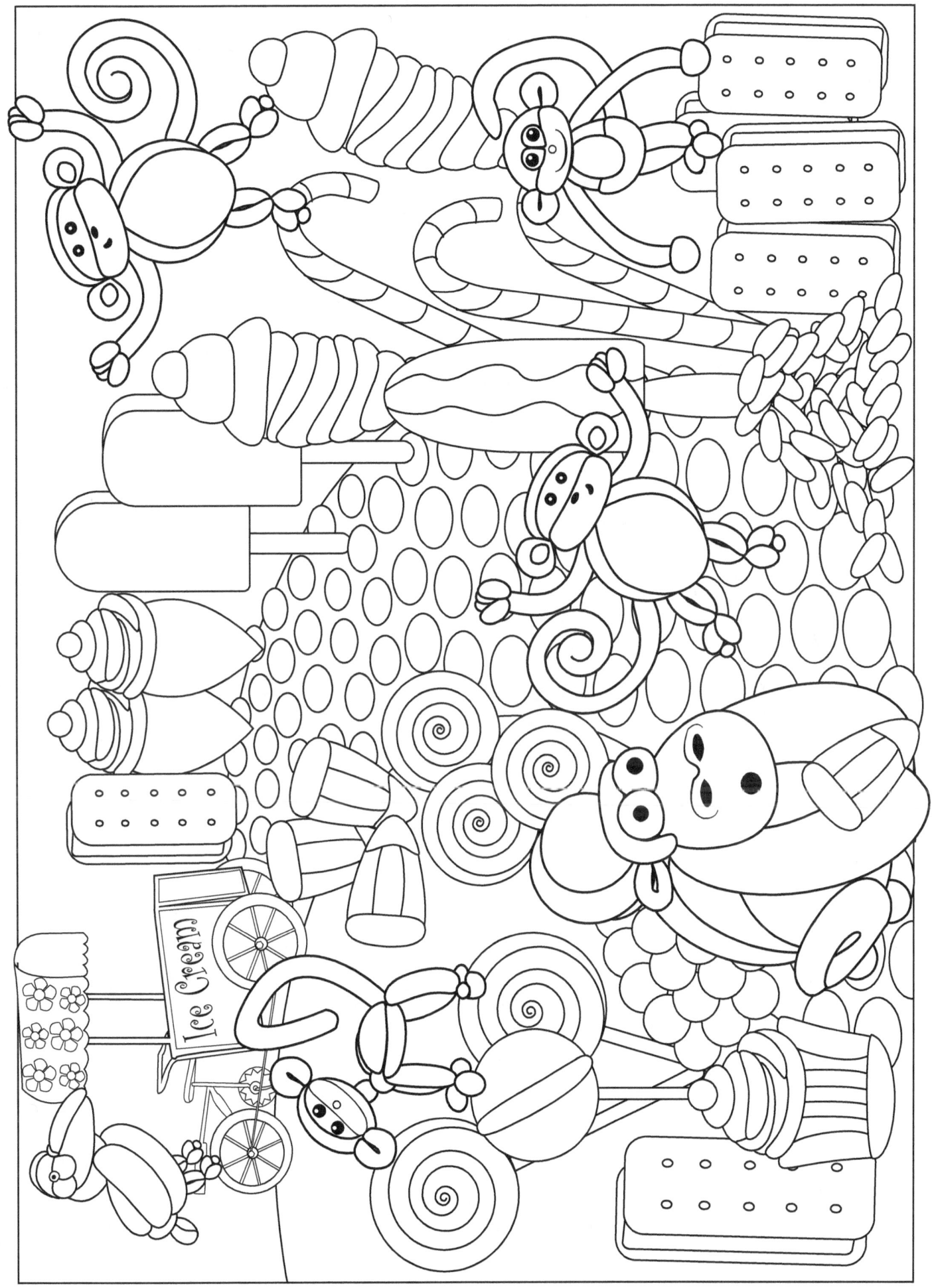

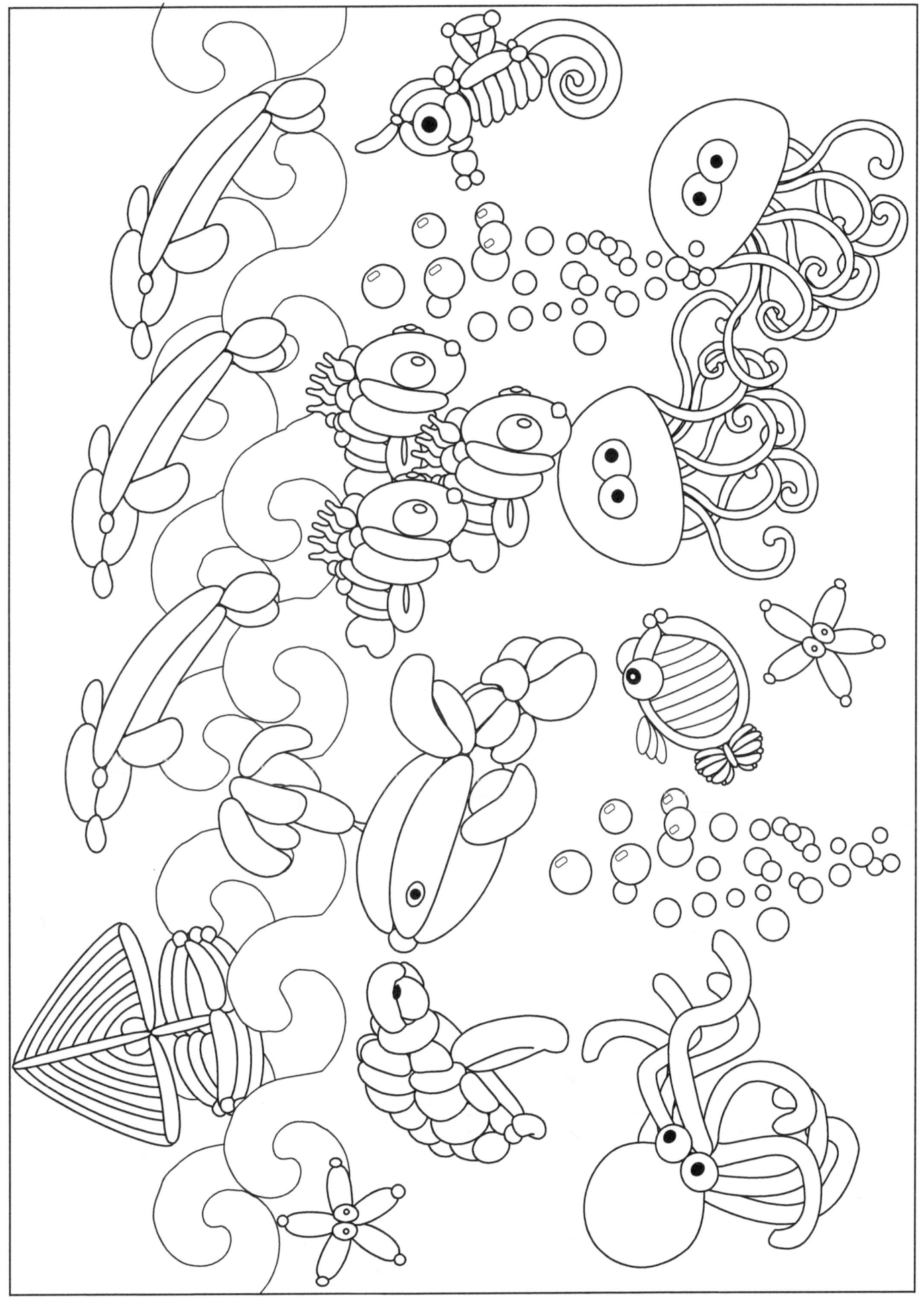

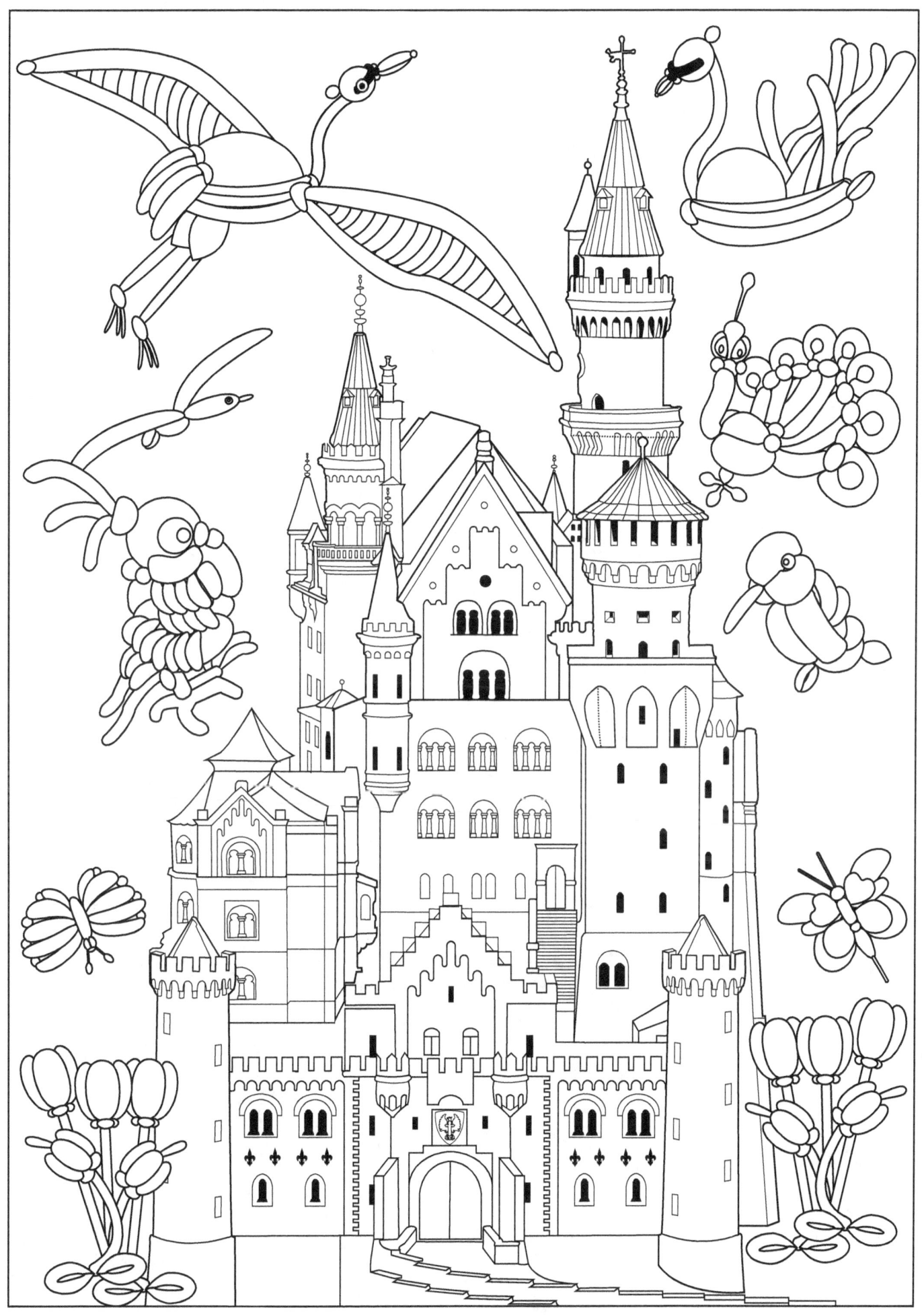

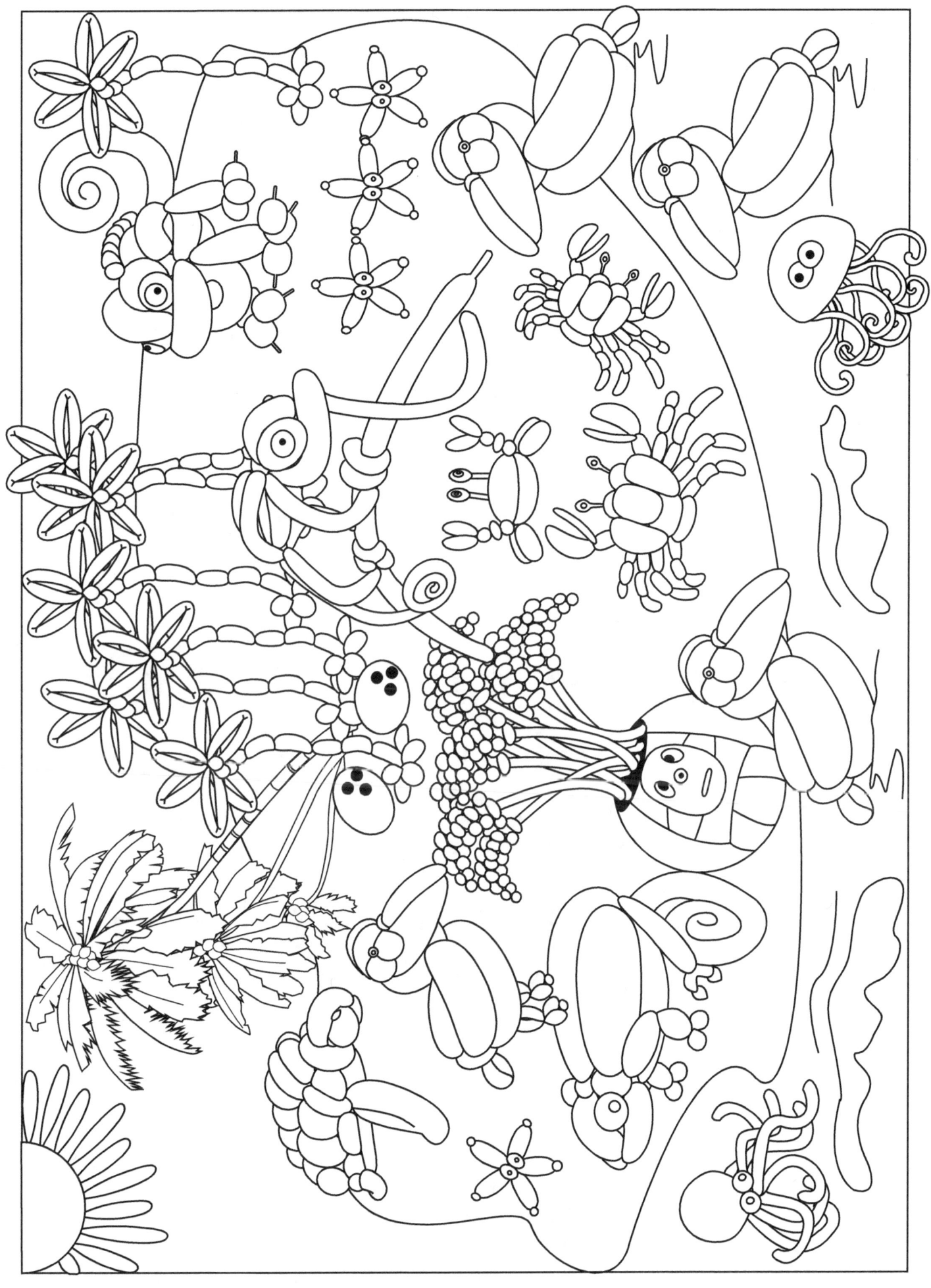

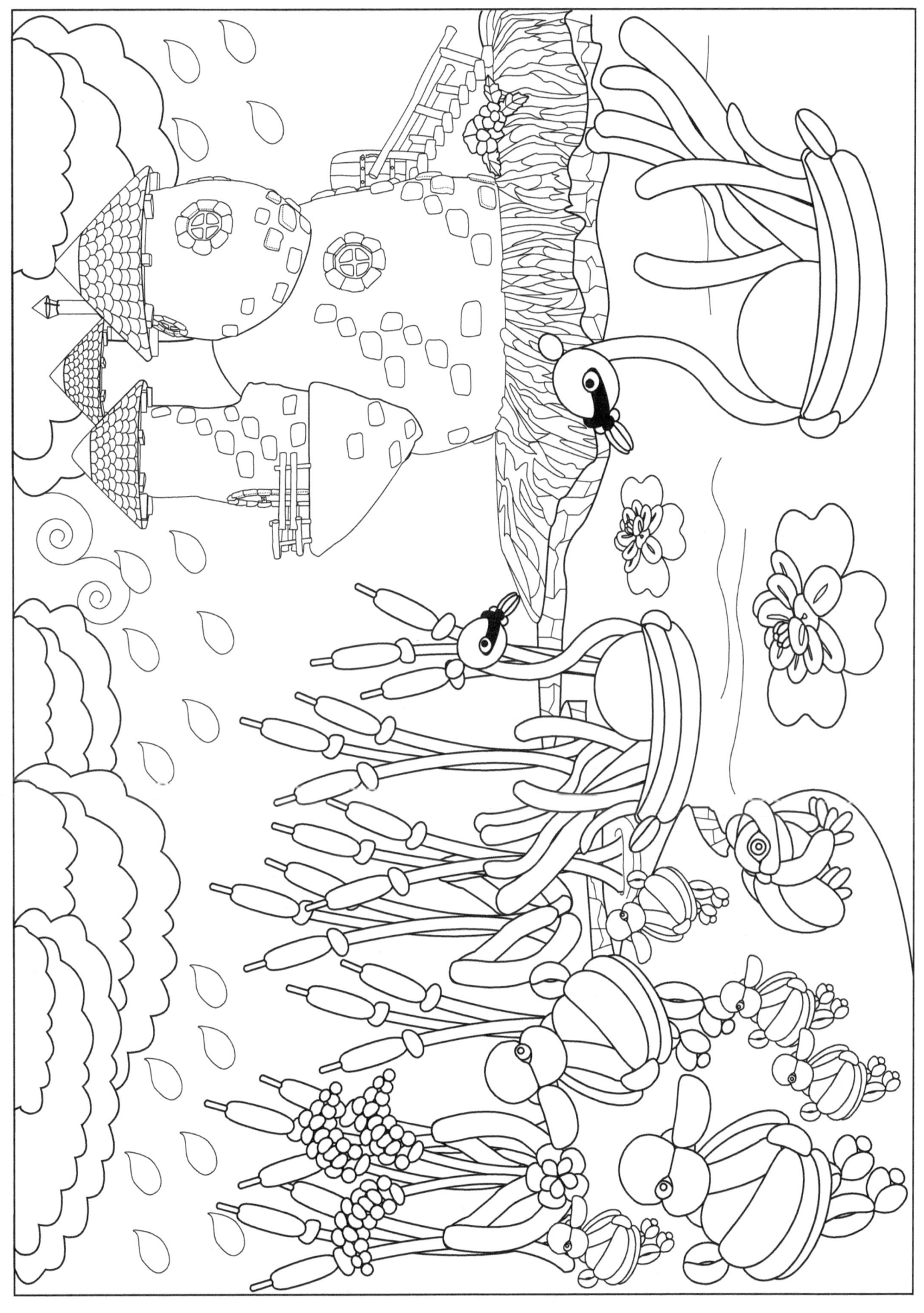

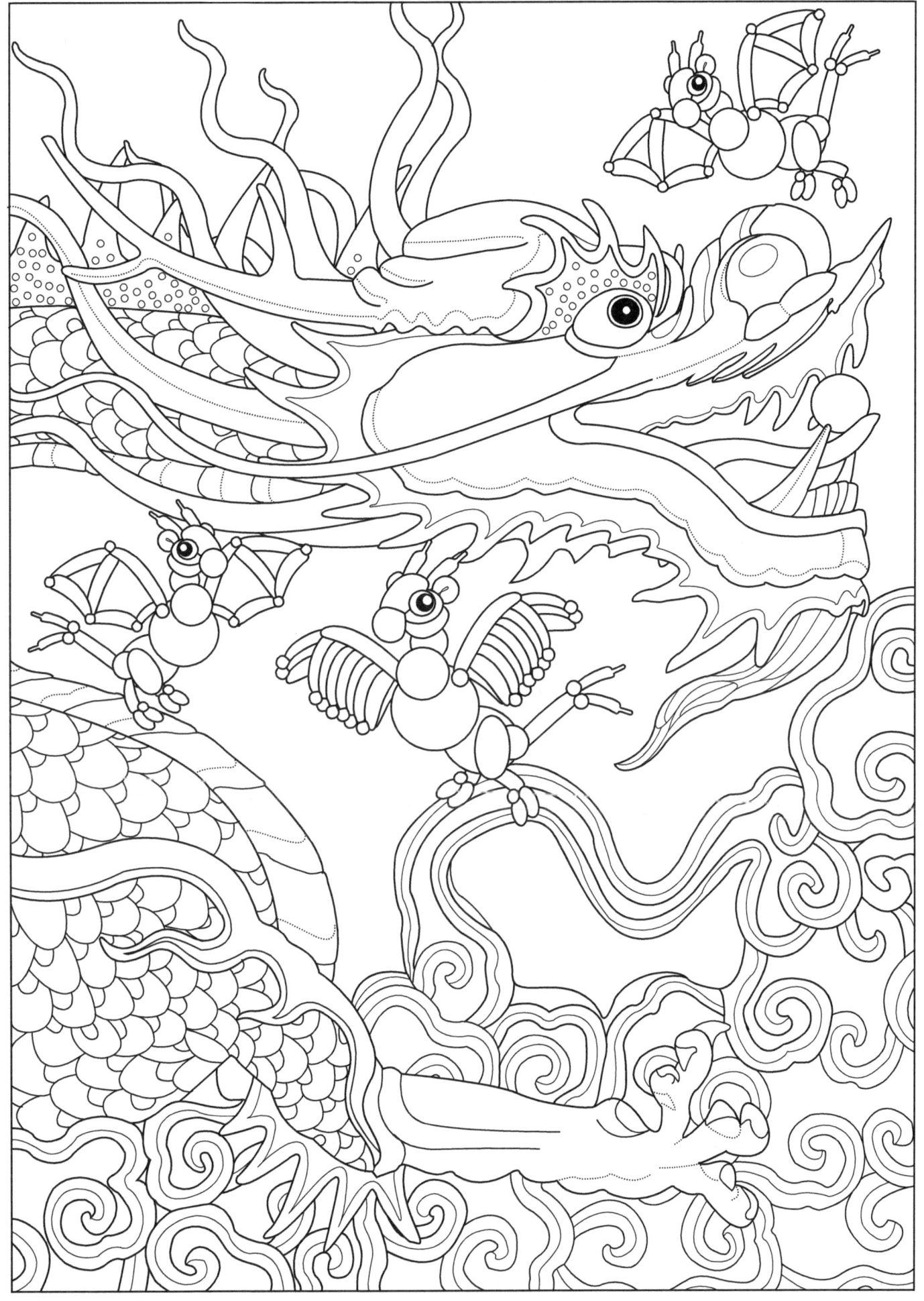

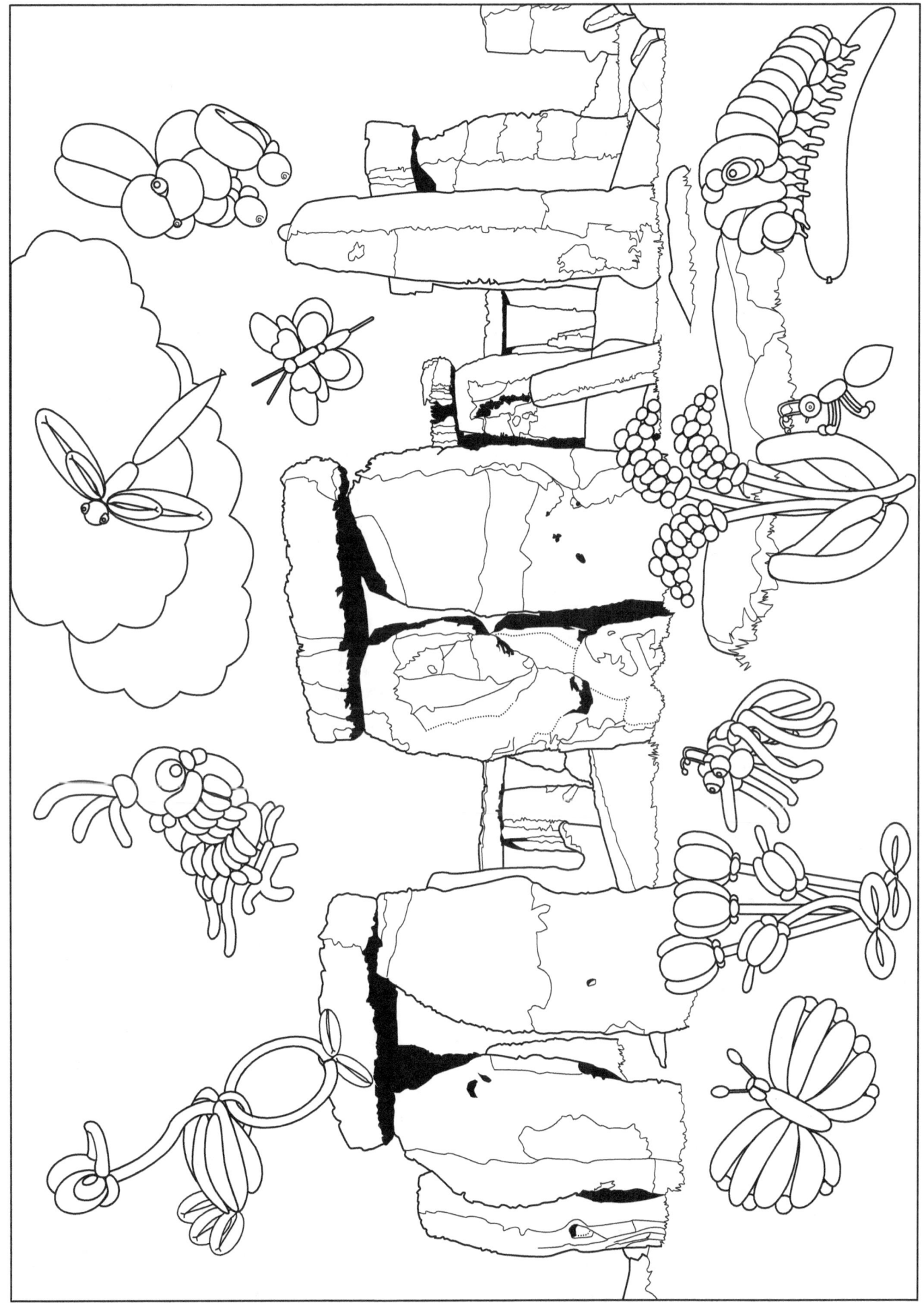

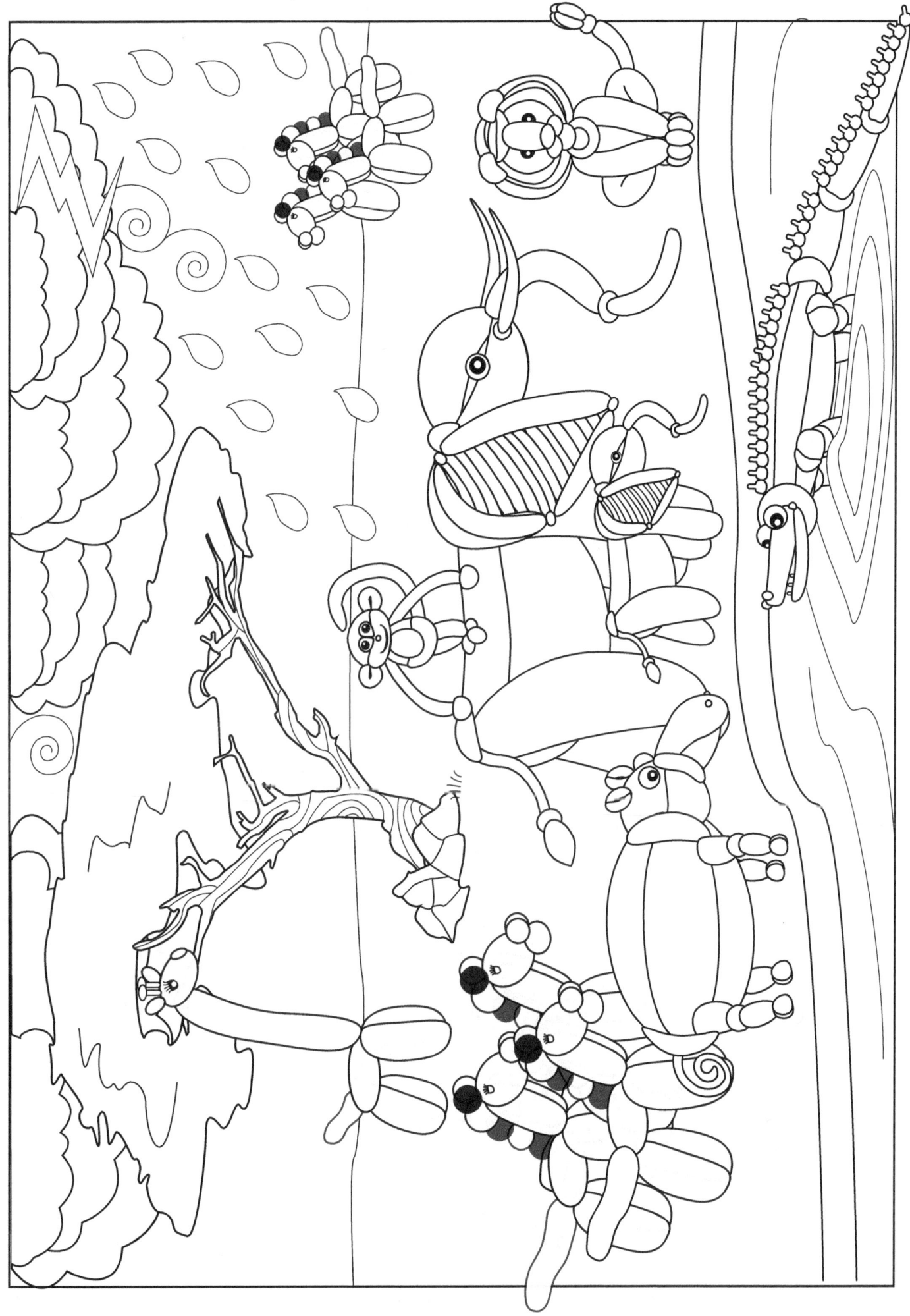

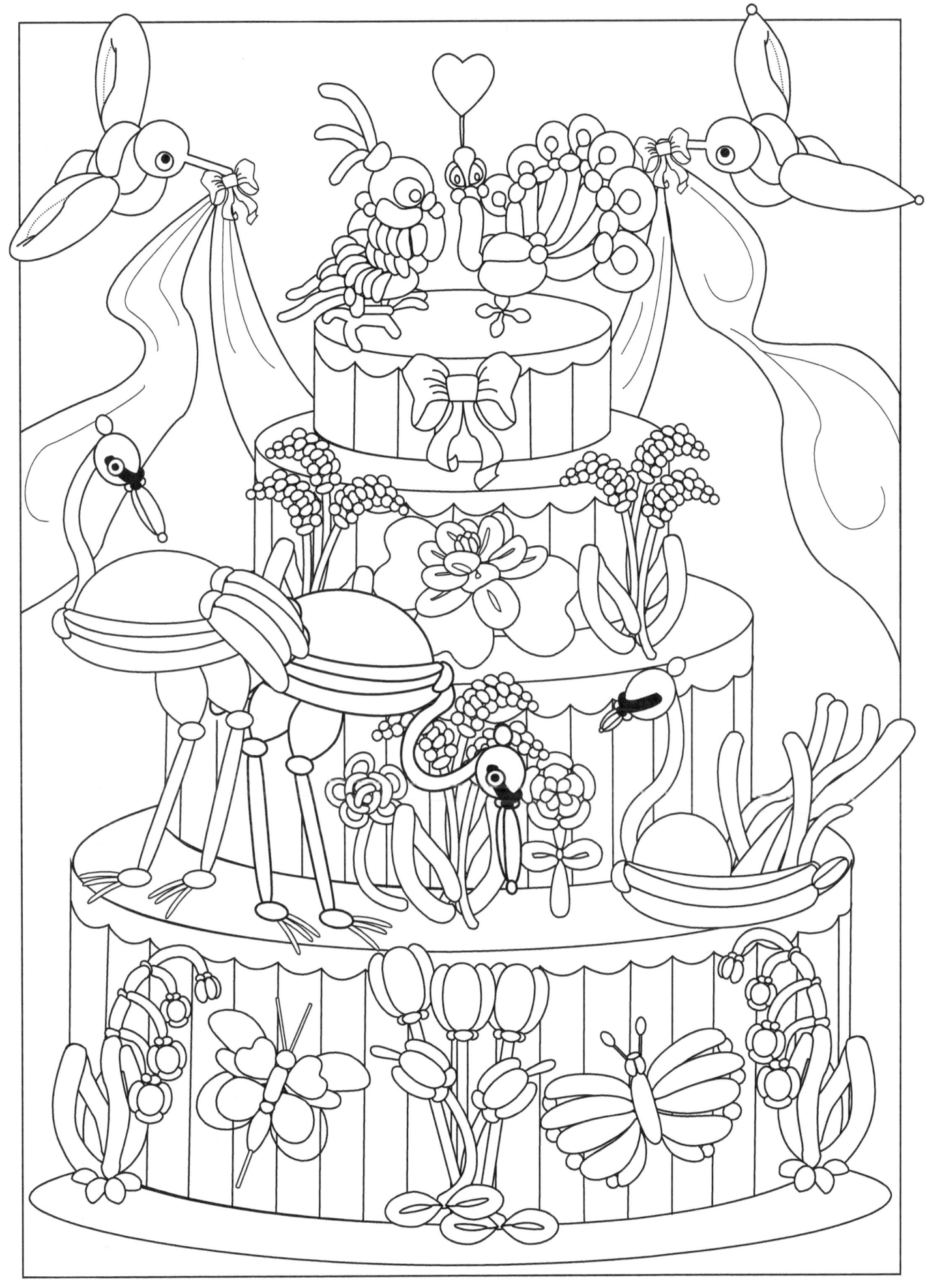

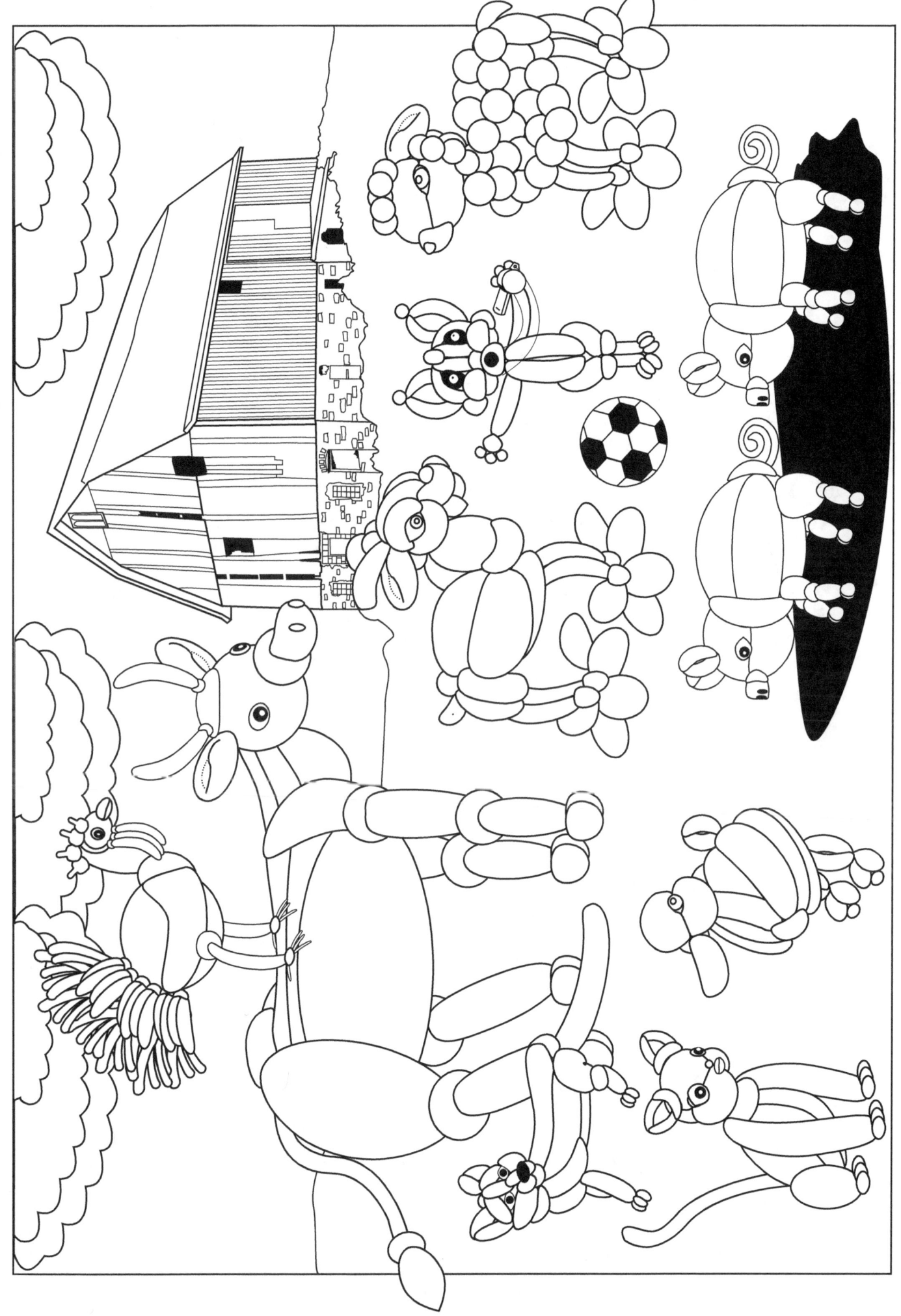

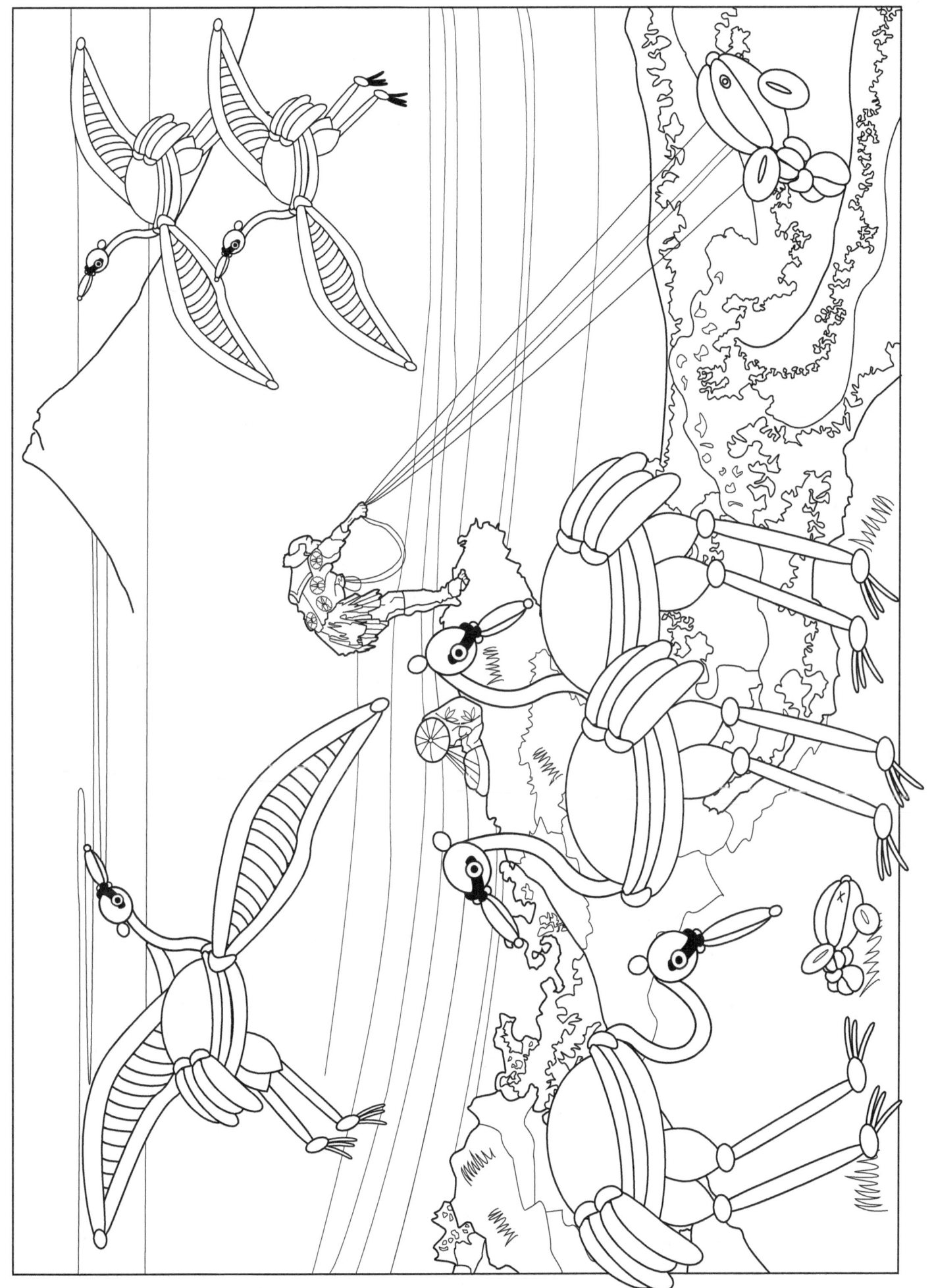

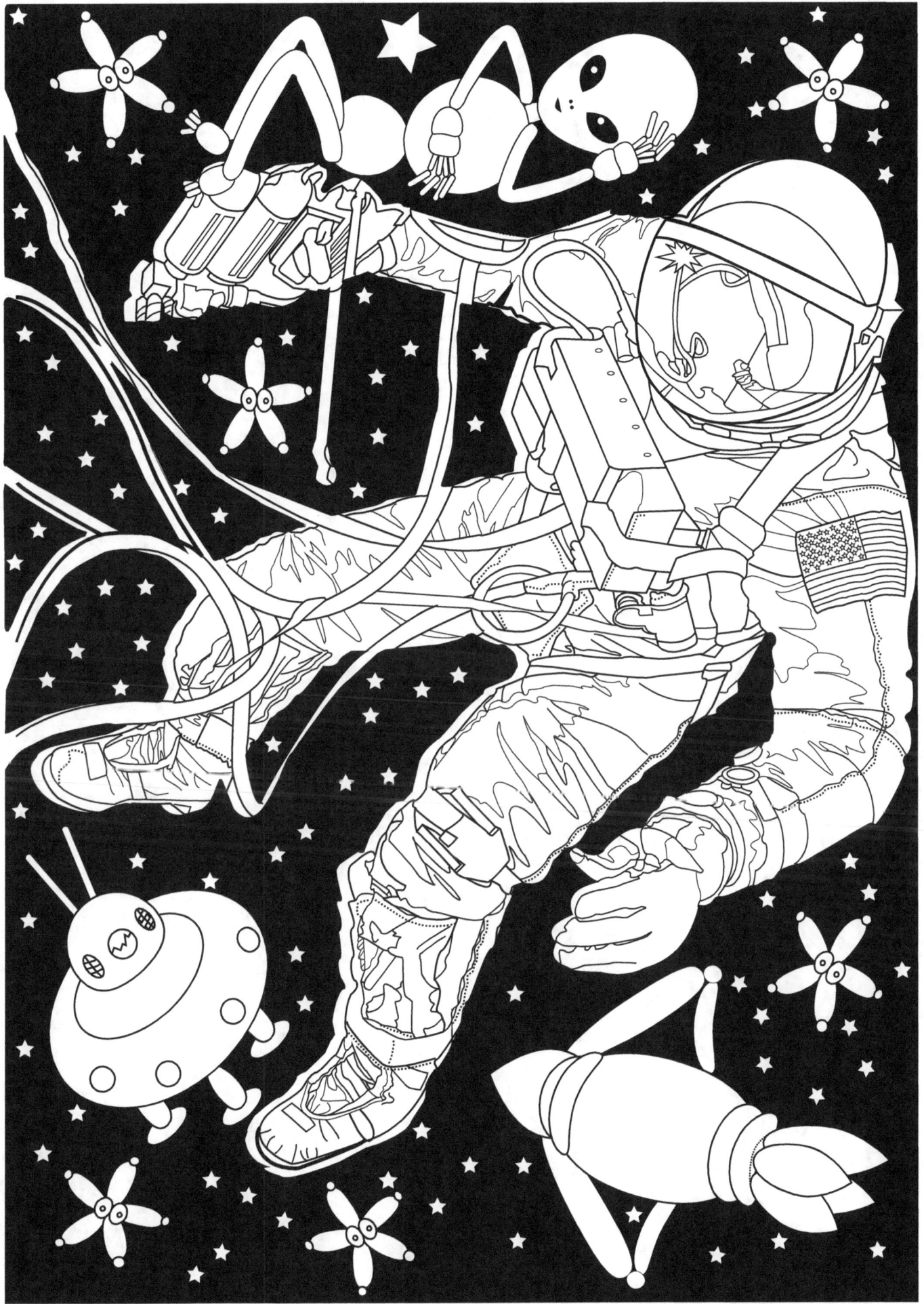

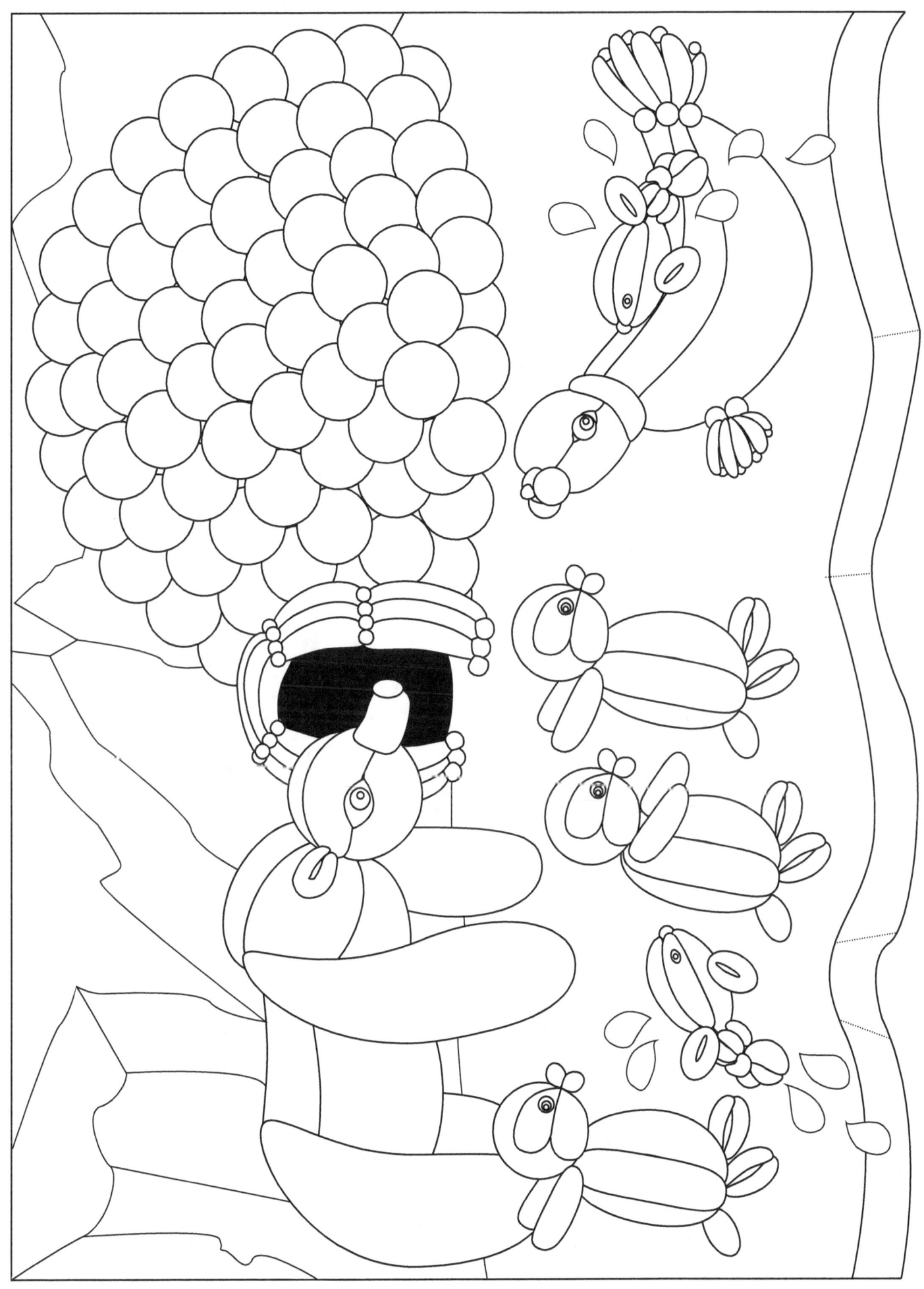

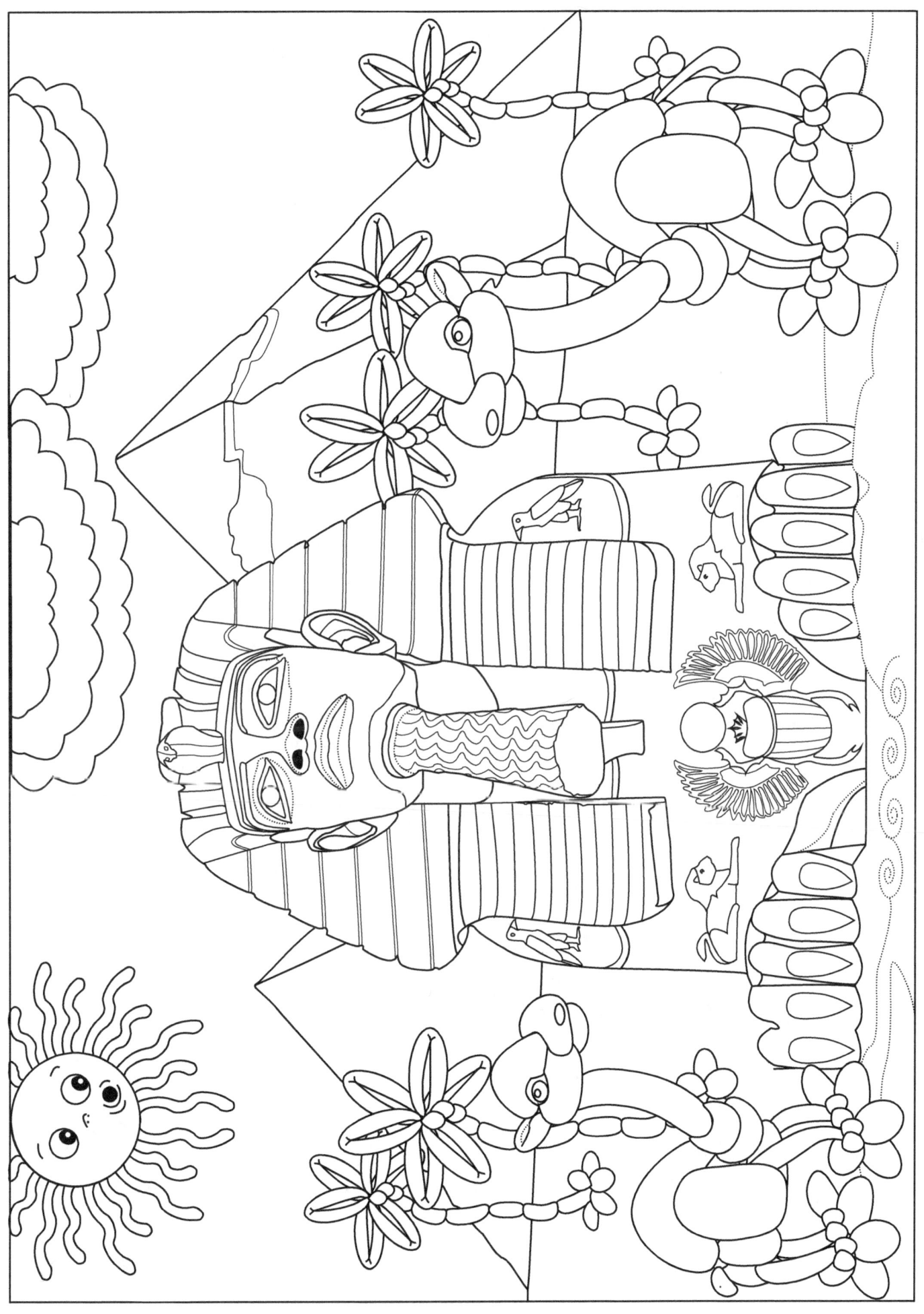

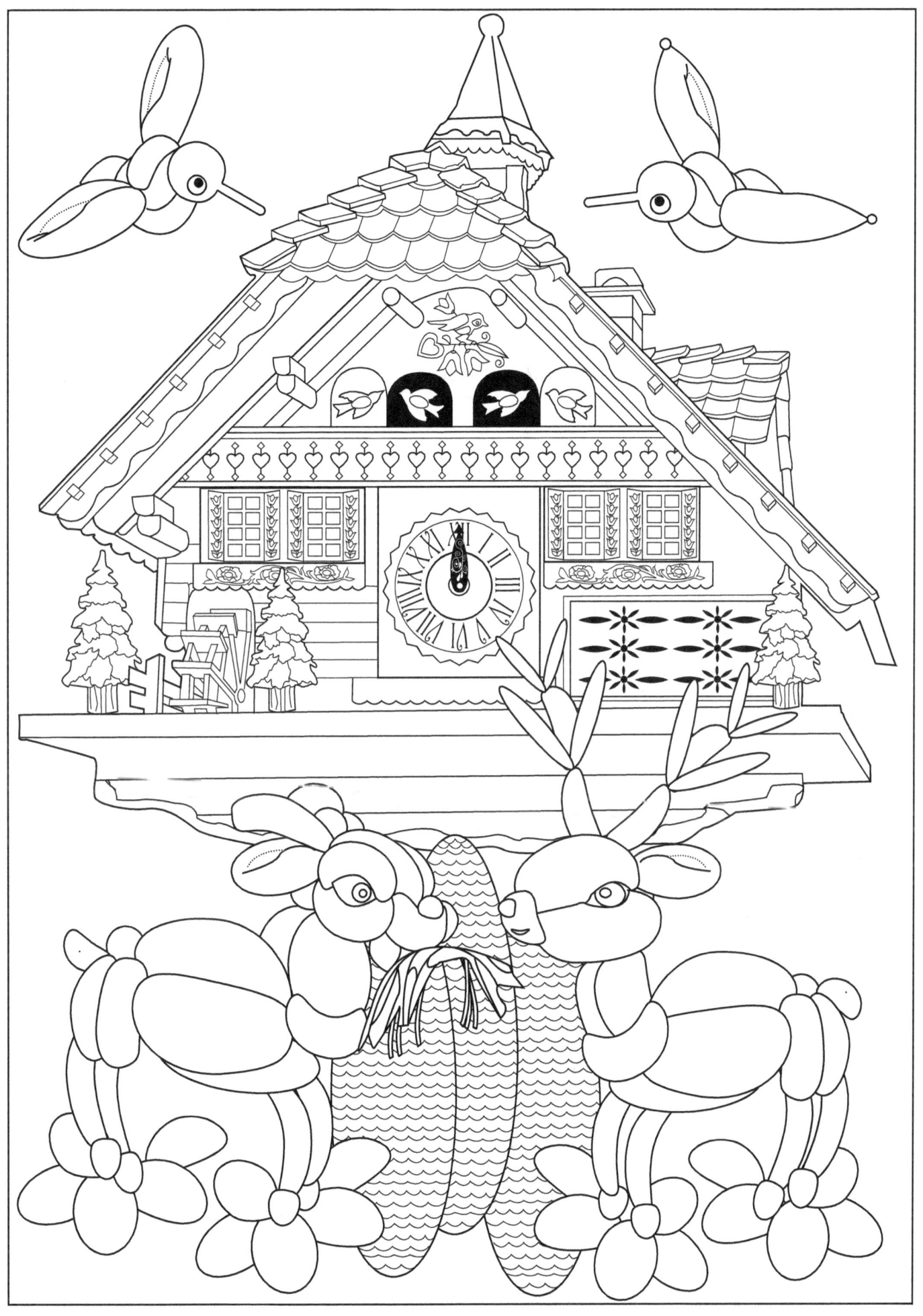

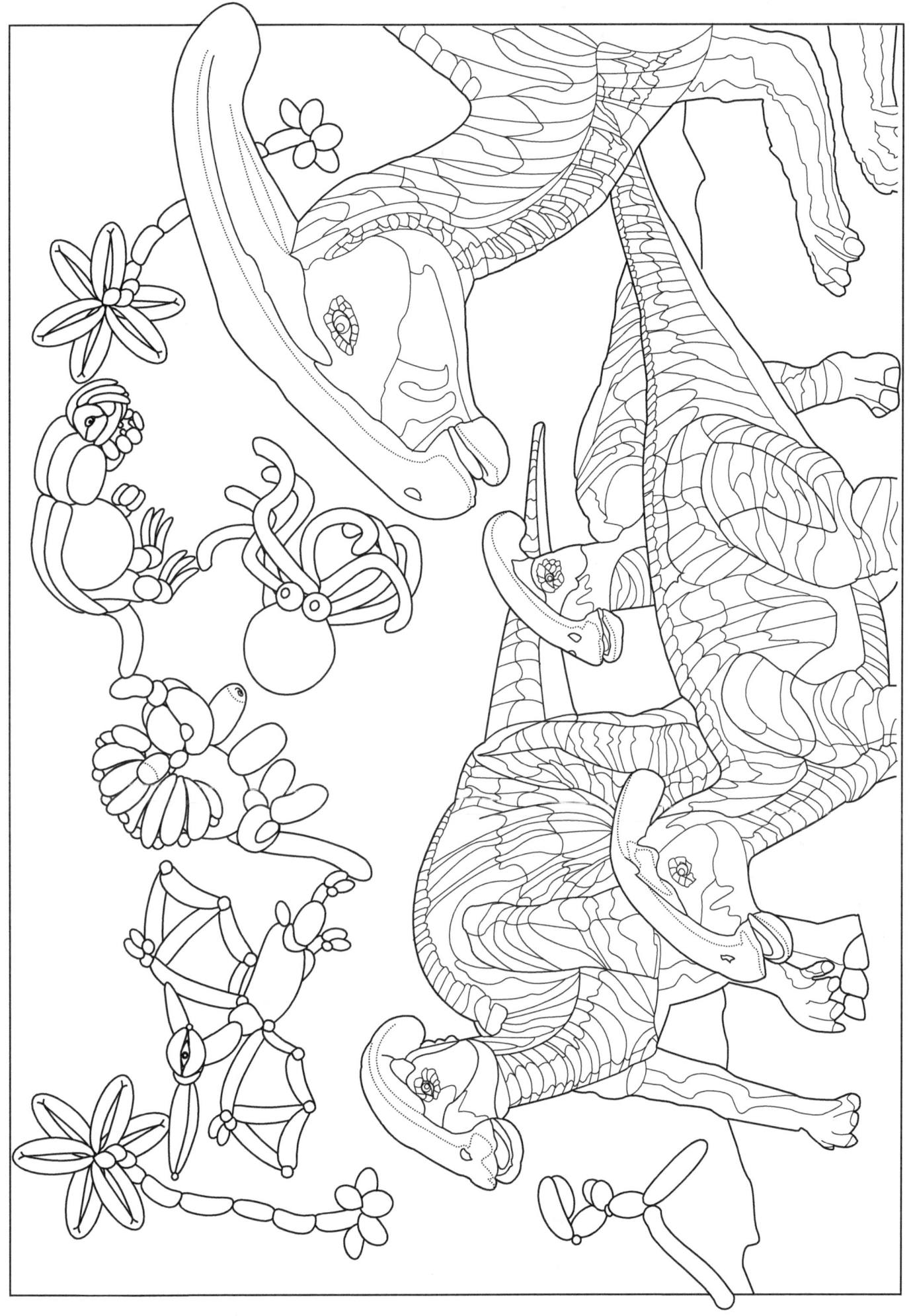

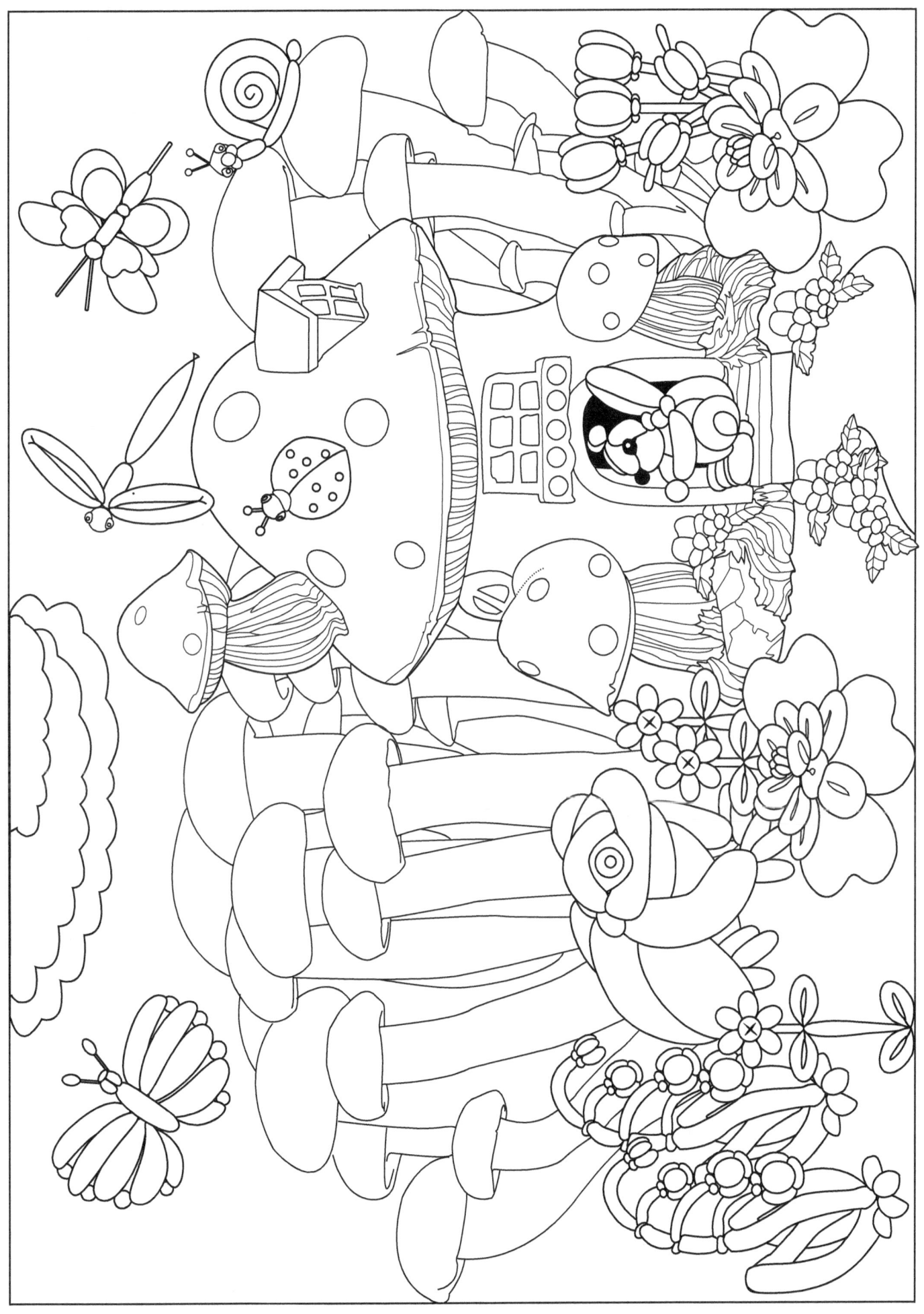

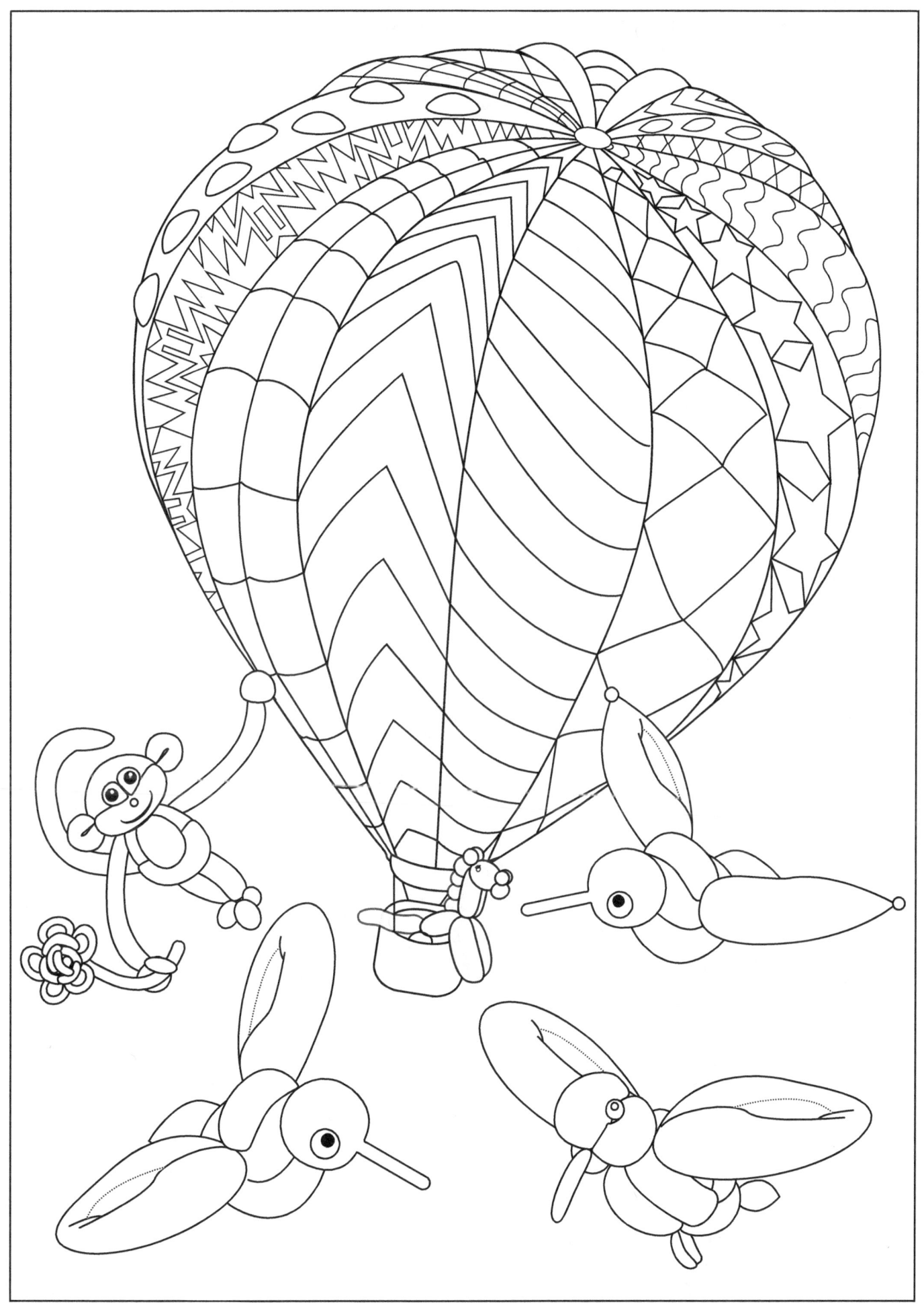

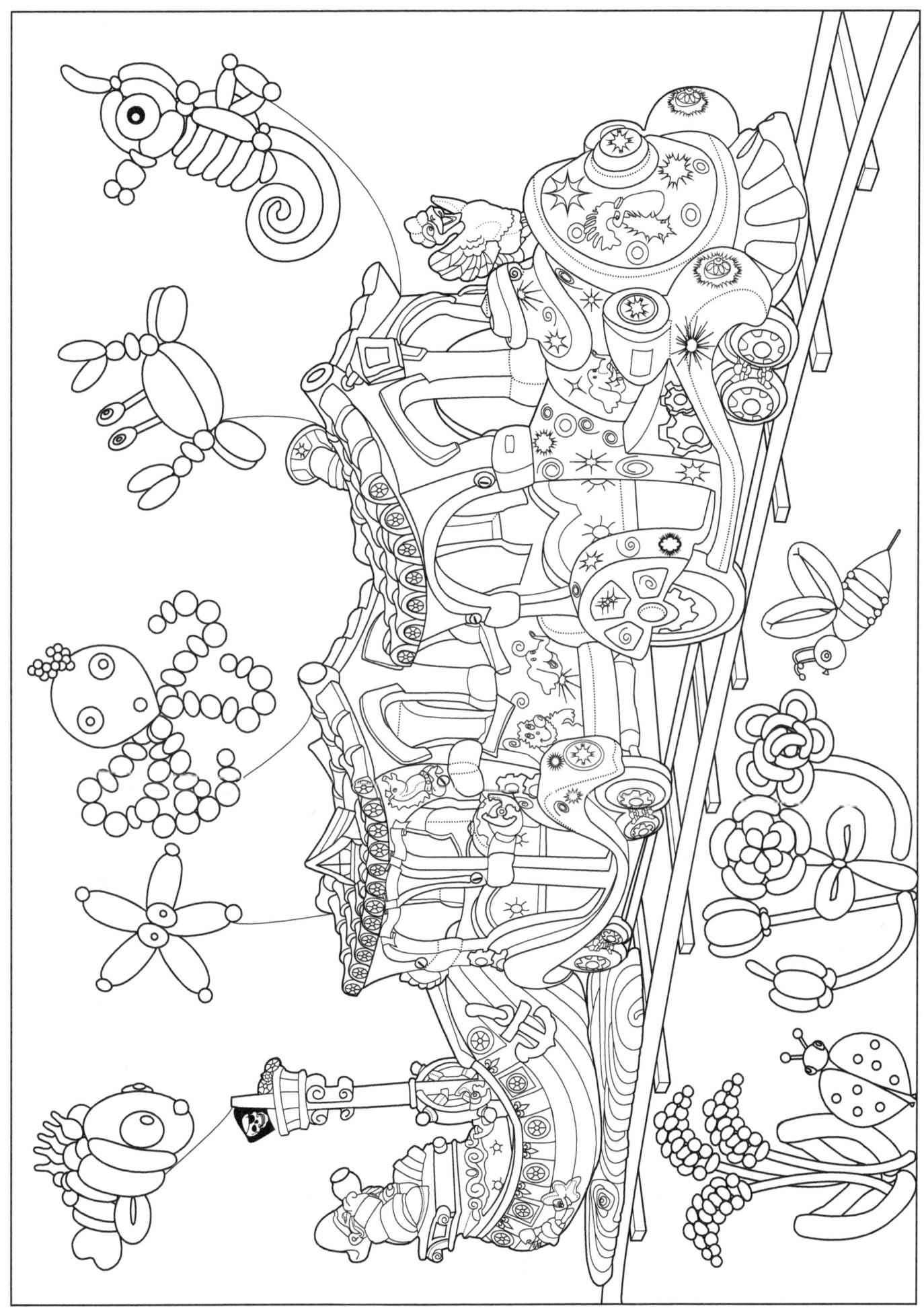

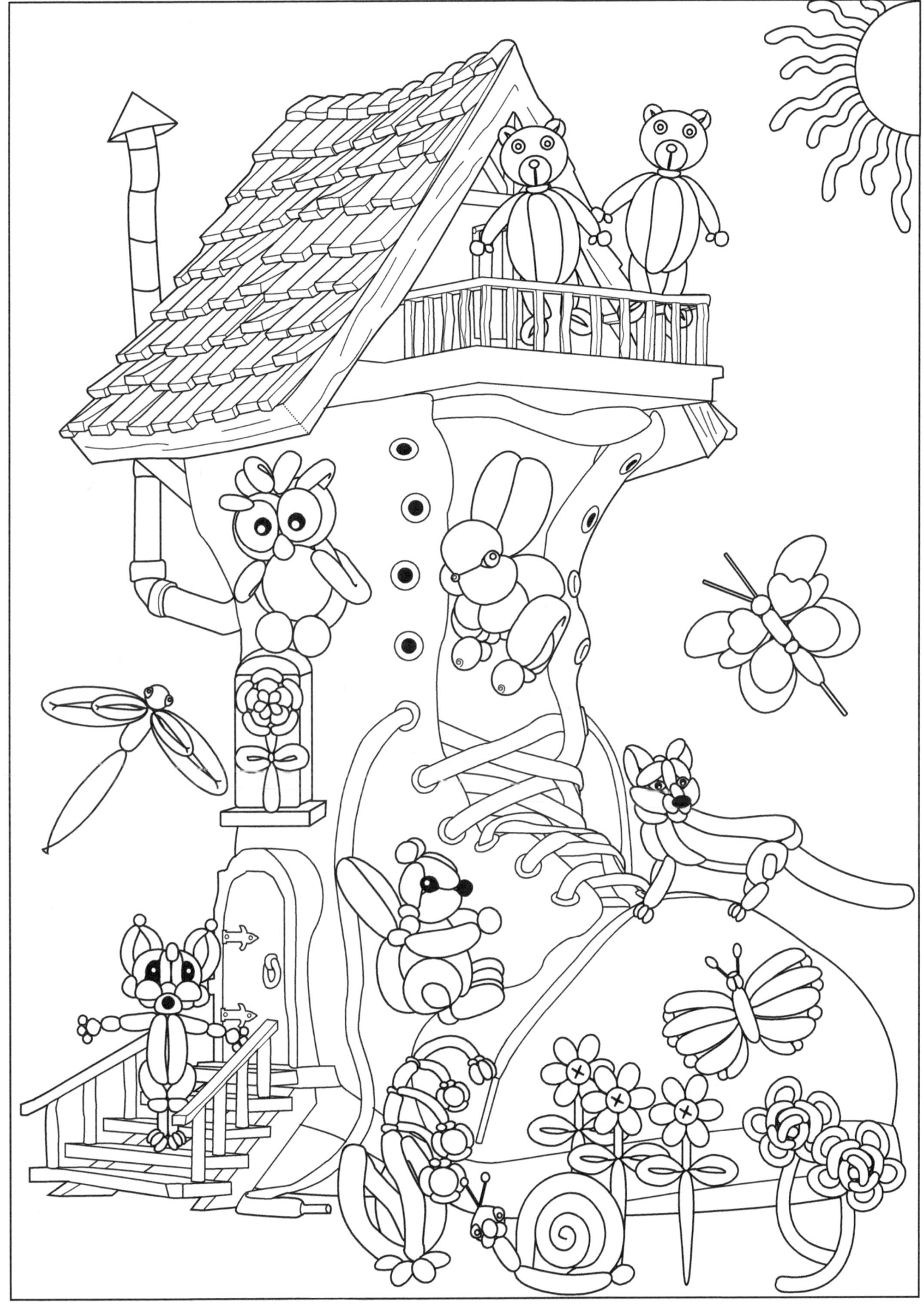

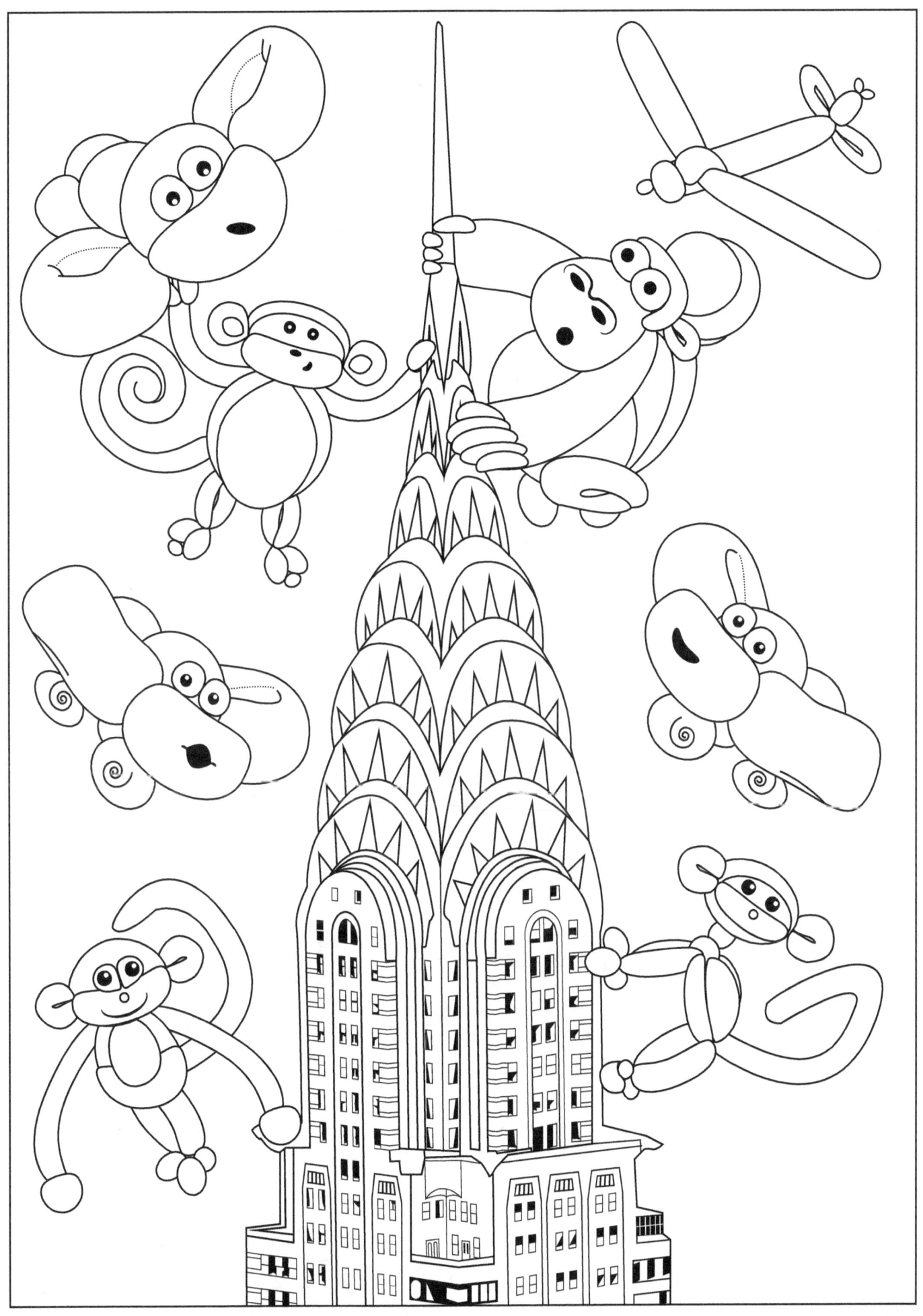

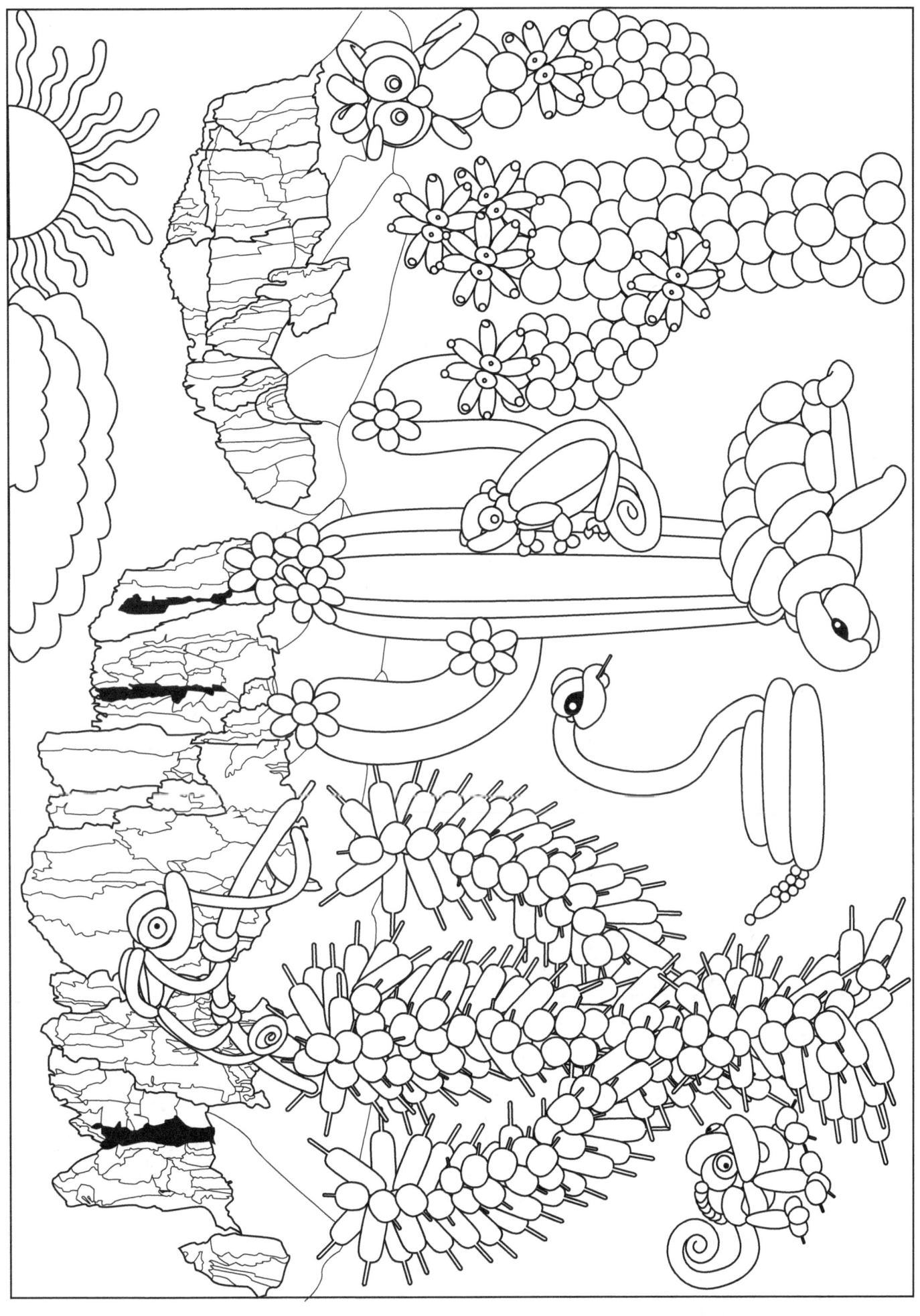

www.ingramcontent.com/pod-product-compliance
Lightning Source LLC
Chambersburg PA
CBHW080136240526
45468CB00009BA/2459